After the Love is Gone:
Finding Strength in a Loveless Relationship

"In the quiet ache of a fading relationship,
discover the strength to rise again."

Vgdawson

Published by
Second Season Press
Birmingham, Alabama
www.what2buynext.com
ISBN: 978-1-972518-04-5

First Edition: 2026

To those who have felt lost in love but found strength within themselves.

To everyone searching for peace and purpose.

May you find the courage to embrace your worth and live with inner freedom.

Table of Contents

Introduction

Love has a way of drawing us in, promising joy, connection, and a future of shared dreams. For many, relationships are where they invest their deepest hopes, their strongest emotions, and their truest selves.

But what happens when, somewhere along the way, that love fades? When mutual respect crumbles, self-worth wanes, and what was once a source of joy becomes an anchor that weighs us down?

After the Love is Gone is for those who find themselves in the quiet, often lonely space of a loveless relationship. Perhaps you stay out of necessity, with nowhere else to go, or maybe the years have worn away the thought of starting over.

For some, leaving has become a daunting impossibility, time has closed the door, or practical constraints keep it firmly shut. Yet here you are, trying to make peace, to find strength, and to redefine what life looks like beyond love's initial promises.

This book is not about fault or blame but about understanding and acceptance. It's a journey into the quiet resilience it takes to stay when love is gone. Through these pages, we'll explore the gradual erosion of connection, the reasons we choose to stay, and the toll it can take on our minds, hearts, and souls.

We'll also discover ways to find strength in the here and now, embracing a new reality without letting it consume the core of who we are.

If you're here, you're not alone. Many people navigate these uncharted waters, balancing the desire for something more with the practicalities of their current lives.

This book is a companion for those in the silent struggle, a guide to reclaiming self-worth and resilience even within the constraints of a relationship that has lost its love. Together, let's find ways to not only survive but to rediscover a sense of self and, ultimately, a sense of peace.

Welcome to After the Love is Gone. Let's walk this path toward resilience, acceptance, and inner strength—together.

Chapter 1: Recognizing the Fade: When Love Slowly Slips Away

Love rarely disappears overnight; more often, it fades gradually, like a sunset sinking beneath the horizon. In the beginning, relationships thrive on connection, excitement, and mutual respect. Conversations flow easily, and you feel understood, seen, and valued.

But over time, small cracks may begin to show. Maybe it's the casual dismissiveness that creeps into your partner's tone or the quiet absence of once-frequent laughter. Eventually, the warmth you felt fades, leaving behind a quiet, aching emptiness that's hard to name but impossible to ignore.

Early Signs of Emotional Distance

The first signs of love fading are often subtle, so much so that many people brush them off, chalking them up to the "normal" progression of a long-term relationship. Busy lives, shifting priorities, and the weight of daily routines can all contribute to a disconnect that feels, at first, temporary.

You tell yourself it's just a phase, but deep down, something has changed. Perhaps your partner no longer shares their day with you or seems disinterested in yours. Affection feels routine, and the spontaneity that once defined your bond is lost.

There's also the small but telling silence when something meaningful happens in your life, and your partner is the last to hear. That moment you once shared eagerly with each other now feels like an obligation, as though connection itself has become something you must remind each other to fulfill.

For some, this distance is hard to pinpoint. It's not one glaring issue but a thousand small ones that accumulate over time.

From Connection to Routine

Another hallmark of fading love is the shift from genuine connection to mere routine. In the early days, you might have gone out of your way to surprise each other, share hobbies, or engage in deep conversations. But now, routine is the main thing holding you together.

You go through the motions, dinner, chores, obligations, but the heart and spontaneity are gone. It feels less like sharing a life and more like checking boxes.

Routine can be both comforting and imprisoning. Some couples settle into it as a natural phase, while others find it numbing. You may wake up one day and realize it's been months since you've truly connected.

The topics you once passionately discussed become points of tension or, worse, avoidance.

When love fades, it can feel as though the person you once knew so intimately has become a stranger sharing your home. But because the changes happened gradually, this shift can be difficult to articulate or even acknowledge.

The Weight of Unspoken Resentment

Over time, resentment builds in ways you may not immediately recognize. Little disappointments accumulate into a quiet, almost invisible frustration.

These unspoken resentments may emerge in passive-aggressive remarks, short tempers, or an unwillingness to make the same compromises that once came naturally.

It might be a forgotten anniversary, a disagreement left unresolved, or a series of unmet needs. The trust that once formed the bedrock of your relationship begins to crack under the weight of these unresolved hurts.

This stage of fading love is often characterized by avoidance. To prevent conflict, you avoid certain topics or situations, but each avoidance leads to greater distance.

Eventually, you may begin to avoid each other, emotionally retreating to avoid the painful reality of a bond weakened by time and silence.

This is how emotional walls are built, brick by brick, without intending to, until you look up one day and find yourselves isolated from each other.

The Loss of Affection and Physical Intimacy

When love fades, affection is often one of the first things to go. Once, a simple touch or affectionate glance would brighten your day, but now those gestures feel absent.

Physical intimacy becomes a routine task rather than a source of connection, or it disappears altogether. Where once there was a warmth that felt genuine, there is now an uncomfortable silence, or worse, a feeling of obligation.

In some relationships, the fading of physical affection doesn't come from a lack of desire but from a deeper sense of disconnection. When emotional intimacy fades, physical closeness can feel forced or hollow.

This lack of affection is painful because it underscores the loneliness of your situation. It can make you question whether your partner sees you at all, much less values you.

Questioning Your Worth and Place in the Relationship

As love fades, many people begin to doubt themselves and their worth.

You may wonder what you could have done differently or if something about you changed to make your partner drift away. You search for reasons, replay conversations, and second-guess decisions, all while feeling your sense of self slip.

When love fades, it's easy to internalize the loss, to believe it reflects something flawed or unworthy in yourself.

However, this questioning can be a pivotal moment. It's often here that people start to see the truth of the situation: sometimes, love fades not because of failure or lack, but because relationships evolve and change.

At some point, you have to face the possibility that this is no longer the relationship you thought it was, and that realization, as difficult as it is, can be the first step toward understanding where you stand.

Choosing to Acknowledge the Fade

The final part of recognizing when love fades is deciding to truly acknowledge it. This isn't about blame or judgment, but about accepting what is. Admitting that the relationship has lost its spark can be painful, especially when there is still a part of you that remembers how good it once was.

But coming to terms with the truth frees you to take your next step, whether that means working to rebuild what has been lost or finding peace in what remains.

Acknowledging the fade is difficult, but it is also liberating. It allows you to see the relationship for what it is today, not what it once was or what you wish it could be.

And from that place of honesty, you can begin to understand what staying means for you and whether you have the strength to either rebuild the relationship or find fulfillment on your own terms.

In Chapter 1, we explore the gradual process by which love fades within a long-term relationship. Unlike sudden breakups, this type of emotional distance builds quietly, often unnoticed at first.

We examine the subtle shifts, like emotional withdrawal, loss of affection, and the transition from genuine connection to routine, that signal a weakening bond.

These small changes, when left unaddressed, contribute to deeper emotional walls and an accumulation of unspoken resentment.

As love fades, partners may experience self-doubt, questioning their own worth and role in the relationship.

The chapter encourages acknowledging the reality of this distance, not as a failure, but as an honest reflection of where the relationship stands.

This acceptance can be the first step toward finding clarity, whether that means working to rebuild the relationship or seeking fulfillment within the new dynamic.

Recognizing the fade empowers individuals to understand their reality and opens the door to finding strength, even in a situation where love has grown distant.

"The Last Kiss I Remember" – Dana, Age 52

Dana remembers exactly when she stopped waiting up for Marcus to come home. After twenty-six years of marriage, their once-nightly tradition of bedtime chats gave way to silence, separate screens, and stiff goodnights. The last kiss she remembers, truly remembers, was two Christmases ago. Now, she pours two cups of coffee out of habit, not desire. And though they still share a home, they haven't shared laughter in what feels like a lifetime. "We didn't fall out of love all at once," she said. "It just… left. Quietly. And neither of us chased after it."

Can you relate to any part of this story?

What would reclaiming your voice look like today, even in a small way?

"When love fades, where do you find strength?"

Chapter 2: Silent Compromises: How We Lose Ourselves in Love

Love has a way of reshaping our lives. In a healthy relationship, it can help us grow, bringing out the best parts of who we are.

But sometimes, we make subtle compromises in the name of love that, over time, become much more significant than we intended. These silent compromises are often small and well-intentioned, a favorite hobby we stop pursuing, a friend we see less often, or a dream we set aside "just for now."

But as they accumulate, they can change the core of who we are, and we may wake up one day feeling lost and unsure of our own identity.

The Allure of Sacrifice in the Early Stages

In the beginning, compromise can feel like a natural part of love. We want to please our partners, meet them halfway, and create a shared life. Small sacrifices, like spending more time together or prioritizing the other person's interests, can be acts of love.

Early on, it's easy to dismiss these changes as temporary, believing that balance will eventually return. We give up certain things willingly, hoping that the depth of connection will outweigh any individual sacrifices.

But it's important to recognize when these sacrifices begin to alter our sense of self. Over time, we can begin to abandon our hobbies, our routines, and even our values in small, almost invisible ways.

As the relationship progresses, these changes become less about sharing life and more about accommodating the other person's needs, sometimes at the expense of our own.

The Erosion of Personal Boundaries

Silent compromises often involve a gradual erosion of personal boundaries. In love, we may feel that boundaries are unnecessary or even counterproductive.

After all, we're building a life together, why should there be walls?

But healthy boundaries aren't walls; they are guidelines for maintaining a strong sense of self within a partnership. Without them, we risk losing ourselves in the other person's needs, expectations, and desires.

Imagine the small things you used to prioritize for yourself that you now feel guilty for enjoying. Perhaps you used to take time each weekend for a favorite hobby, or you valued an hour of solitude each morning. Over time, these personal boundaries may blur, leaving you feeling uneasy but unsure why.

These silent compromises add up, leading you to feel you've let go of pieces of yourself that once brought you joy or centered you.

Self-Worth Becomes Intertwined with the Relationship

One of the most impactful ways we lose ourselves in love is when our self-worth becomes tightly intertwined with the relationship. In the early stages, it may feel empowering to be someone's "better half."

But when our identity is fully wrapped up in being a partner, it can erode our ability to feel valuable outside of that role. When we compromise too much, we may begin to see ourselves only through the lens of the relationship, evaluating our worth based on our partner's approval or happiness.

Over time, we might begin to measure ourselves by our ability to keep the relationship intact, to make our partner happy, or to avoid conflict.

This leads to a loss of self, as our identity and worth are no longer self-generated but instead are reflections of the relationship's health. When our worth becomes conditional on maintaining harmony in the relationship, we can feel adrift if the connection becomes strained or uncertain.

Suppressing Desires, Dreams, and Opinions

Another silent compromise occurs when we suppress our own desires, dreams, or opinions to avoid rocking the boat. At first, this may seem harmless. We tell ourselves it's better not to bring up certain topics or that our dreams can wait.

Maybe we keep quiet about something we'd love to pursue, like a new career, travel plans, or a big project, because we know it doesn't align with our partner's plans. Over time, we lose sight of these dreams entirely.

Suppressing opinions can be even more damaging because it implies a lack of confidence in our right to be heard. Small disagreements or differing views may feel unimportant enough to ignore at first, but as we begin to silence ourselves consistently, we send ourselves the message that our voice doesn't matter.

Suppressing our desires and opinions leads to resentment, frustration, and, ultimately, a sense of alienation from our own lives.

Fading Friendships and Losing Social Connections

A common silent compromise is distancing ourselves from friends, family, and other social connections.

While it's natural for a new relationship to consume much of our time and energy, isolating ourselves from other relationships can leave us overly dependent on our partner for emotional support.

Friendships and social connections provide perspective and reinforce our sense of self. They remind us of who we are outside of our romantic relationship.

However, as we invest more in our relationship, our social lives often begin to fade. We may feel obligated to choose between spending time with friends or our partner, and eventually, our support network dwindles.

This isolation not only affects our happiness but can also make it harder to recognize if the relationship becomes unbalanced or toxic.

Maintaining connections outside the relationship helps anchor us and provides a reality check, especially if we start to feel we're losing ourselves.

Losing Autonomy in Decision-Making

Decision-making within a relationship should ideally be a shared, balanced process. However, silent compromises can lead one partner to prioritize the other's preferences over their own, creating an uneven dynamic.

Over time, we may begin to defer to our partner's wishes, putting aside our own opinions, even on decisions that deeply affect us. These choices could be as simple as deciding where to go for dinner or as significant as making career or financial decisions.

When we consistently yield to our partner's preferences, it undermines our sense of autonomy. We may feel that we don't have a true voice or that our opinions are secondary, and this lack of agency contributes to a sense of disconnect from our own lives.

In a healthy relationship, both partners should feel empowered to make choices, knowing that their voice matters and their individual needs are respected.

The Awakening: Realizing What We've Lost

At some point, many people experience an awakening where they realize just how much of themselves they've compromised. This realization may come after months or even years, perhaps sparked by a simple reminder of an old passion, a long-lost friend reaching out, or even a moment of unexpected solitude.

It can be painful to recognize how many small parts of ourselves we've surrendered in the name of keeping the relationship steady.

This awakening, however, is also an opportunity. It can be the first step toward reclaiming a sense of self, rebuilding boundaries, and reestablishing individual values and goals. Recognizing what we've lost doesn't mean blaming ourselves or regretting our choices.

 Instead, it can be a call to remember who we are and to find ways to honor our own needs within the relationship. If approached with compassion and understanding, this process can lead to renewed self-respect and a healthier, more balanced connection.

In this chapter, we explore how silent compromises, though often made with the best intentions, can gradually erode our sense of self. These small acts of self-sacrifice, giving up hobbies, distancing ourselves from friends, deferring decisions, accumulate until we begin to feel as if we've lost our identity.

Recognizing this pattern can be a powerful step toward reclaiming autonomy and understanding that a healthy relationship should enhance, not overshadow, our individuality.

This chapter aims to shed light on these compromises and encourage readers to evaluate which sacrifices are healthy and which ones may be slowly distancing them from their true selves.

"I Became His Mirror" – Janelle, Age 40

Janelle used to dance. She taught Zumba, sang loudly while cooking, and hosted Sunday dinners. Over time, her partner criticized those things as "too much." So she muted herself, literally and figuratively. She stopped playing music in the house, stopped going out, and slowly disappeared behind his routines. "I didn't even realize I was shrinking," she said. "Until my own reflection felt like a stranger." It wasn't one big compromise; it was a thousand small ones.

Can you relate to any part of this story?

What would reclaiming your voice look like today, even in a small way?

"When Love Stays, but the Feeling Leaves"

Chapter 3: The Cost of Staying: Emotional, Physical, and Mental Toll

When love fades and the spark of a relationship dwindles, staying can take a significant toll, emotionally, physically, and mentally. Although the decision to remain may stem from loyalty, fear of change, or a lack of options, the choice can weigh heavily.

Often, the costs become apparent only over time, manifesting in subtle yet profound ways. In this chapter, we'll examine the multifaceted impact of staying in a loveless relationship, acknowledging the effects on self-worth, mental clarity, physical health, and overall well-being.

Recognizing these costs is essential for understanding why the choice to stay comes with a price and, ultimately, for finding ways to cope and regain strength.

The Emotional Weight of Unfulfilled Love

Emotionally, a loveless relationship can feel like carrying an invisible burden. The absence of affection and meaningful connection often leads to feelings of loneliness, despair, and even rejection.

Each day, individuals in this position may face the quiet disappointment of unmet expectations and the emotional distance that has come to define the relationship.

They may long for companionship, empathy, or support but find that these needs go unaddressed, leading to a deep-seated sadness.

This emotional weight often manifests as feelings of self-doubt, guilt, and shame.

The constant question of "why am I not enough?" or "why can't things be different?" may linger.

People in loveless relationships often internalize the situation, blaming themselves rather than recognizing the larger, mutual dynamics at play. This self-blame can become a destructive cycle that reinforces feelings of inadequacy and worthlessness.

Physical Health and the Body's Reaction to Prolonged Stress

Our bodies often mirror the state of our emotions, and staying in a loveless relationship can have a noticeable effect on physical health.

The stress of staying where we no longer feel valued, respected, or cared for can lead to chronic stress, a well-known factor in a wide array of health issues.

Elevated stress hormones, like cortisol, can disrupt sleep patterns, weaken the immune system, and increase the risk of high blood pressure, heart disease, and digestive issues.

Chronic stress can also lead to changes in appetite and energy levels. Some may find themselves overeating or under-eating, leading to weight gain or loss.

Over time, these physical symptoms can create a feedback loop where the body's struggles exacerbate feelings of helplessness and despair, further impacting physical health. Fatigue and frequent illnesses may become a regular part of life, reflecting the body's response to prolonged emotional strain.

Mental Health Challenges: Anxiety and Depression

Mental health is deeply affected when a person feels trapped in a loveless relationship. The constant tension, lack of support, and emotional neglect can lead to mental health issues like anxiety and depression.

For many, waking up each day in a situation that feels unchanging and unfulfilling can create a persistent feeling of dread. They may worry about confrontation, criticism, or even just the silence that has come to define the relationship.

Depression often creeps in subtly, first as a sense of sadness and gradually growing into a pervasive lack of motivation, numbness, or a feeling of being "stuck." Individuals may lose interest in activities they once enjoyed, feel disconnected from the people around them, or struggle to find purpose in daily life.

This kind of despair can lead to isolation, as they may withdraw from friends, family, or even work. Without intervention, this isolation often deepens, making it even harder to seek help or imagine a way out.

The Erosion of Self-Worth and Confidence

Staying in a relationship where love, respect, and affection are absent can severely impact one's self-worth and confidence. Over time, individuals may internalize the neglect they feel, interpreting it as a reflection of their own value.

They may begin to believe that they're unworthy of love or that they're somehow to blame for the relationship's decline. This belief is often reinforced by a partner's criticism, indifference, or manipulation, leading to a diminished sense of self-worth.

Low self-worth makes it difficult to imagine life outside the relationship, and the fear of the unknown can feel paralyzing.

Individuals may find themselves believing that this is the best they can hope for or that they don't deserve anything better. This erosion of confidence can impact other areas of life, from career aspirations to personal goals, creating a ripple effect of missed opportunities and unfulfilled potential.

The Toll on Cognitive Clarity and Decision-Making

The stress and anxiety of staying in a loveless relationship often affect cognitive functions, impairing clarity and decision-making skills. When under constant emotional strain, individuals may struggle to think clearly, find it challenging to make even small decisions, and become overwhelmed by daily tasks.

This mental fog can make it difficult to assess the situation rationally, leading to a cycle of indecision that further entrenches them in the relationship.

Additionally, mental exhaustion from ongoing stress can lead to memory lapses and reduced focus. Tasks that once seemed easy might now feel monumental.

Over time, this cognitive toll can interfere with job performance, social interactions, and the ability to find joy in everyday life.

A diminished capacity for problem-solving can keep individuals feeling stuck, unable to envision a clear path forward or see potential solutions to their situation.

Strained Relationships with Friends and Family

A loveless relationship often extends its effects to relationships outside the romantic one. Friends and family may notice changes in the individual's demeanor, less joy, a withdrawn attitude, or a sense of sadness.

However, it can be challenging for the individual to share their struggles openly, particularly if they feel ashamed of their situation or believe others won't understand. This reluctance can strain these other relationships, leading to isolation or misunderstandings.

Moreover, the emotional exhaustion from the loveless relationship often leaves little energy to invest in friendships or family ties. This withdrawal can cause those closest to them to feel neglected or pushed away.

Over time, social isolation becomes a byproduct of the toll that staying in the relationship takes. Without a support network, it becomes harder to find a perspective outside the relationship, creating a sense of being trapped.

Finding Resilience and Strength in Adversity

While the cost of staying in a loveless relationship is undeniably high, acknowledging these impacts is a vital step toward change and self-empowerment.

Understanding the emotional, physical, and mental toll can lead individuals to examine their own boundaries, values, and needs. Even in difficult circumstances, resilience can be built by finding small ways to reconnect with one's inner self—through journaling, setting personal goals, or pursuing hobbies.

This journey of resilience often involves reclaiming a sense of identity and self-worth separate from the relationship. It's about recognizing that while the situation may feel dire, personal growth and healing are still possible.

Each step taken to address the emotional, physical, and mental toll, whether by reaching out to friends, practicing self-care, or setting new boundaries, can help to restore a sense of agency and hope.

In this chapter, we examine the multifaceted toll that a loveless relationship takes on a person's well-being. Emotionally, the feelings of loneliness and self-doubt can become overwhelming.

Physically, the body may react to chronic stress in ways that affect health and vitality. Mentally, the ongoing strain can cloud clarity, impact decision-making, and contribute to anxiety and depression.

The social costs can also be significant, with friendships and family ties sometimes fraying under the pressure of isolation and emotional exhaustion.

Understanding these costs is essential for those who find themselves in similar situations. Recognizing that staying in a loveless relationship has real consequences can serve as a catalyst for self-reflection and growth.

In the face of these challenges, resilience and strength can emerge, guiding individuals toward greater self-care, renewed clarity, and, ultimately, a path forward, whether that means choosing to stay or deciding to move on.

"The Body Never Lies" — Carmen, Age 57

Carmen's migraines started in her early 50s. At first, she thought it was menopause. Then the chest tightness came. Then the anxiety. She saw doctors, therapists, and specialists.

But nothing changed until one therapist asked a simple question: "Are you emotionally safe at home?" The truth stunned her. Her husband never hit her, but the constant dismissal, sarcasm, and emotional coldness had drained her for decades.

"My body was screaming what I refused to say out loud: I was unhappy, and it was killing me slowly."

Can you relate to any part of this story?

What would reclaiming your voice look like today, even in a small way?

"Surviving the Silence of a Faded Love"

Chapter 4: Reasons We Don't Leave: Fear, Comfort, and Practicality

Deciding to remain in a relationship where love has faded is often a deeply complex choice. It isn't just about how a person feels; it's about weighing fears, comfort, and the realities of practical life.

Many people stay in relationships that no longer serve them, not because they're happy, but because the idea of leaving can feel even more overwhelming. From fear of the unknown to financial concerns, and the comfort of familiarity, the reasons are varied and multi-layered.

In this chapter, we explore the significant factors that hold people back from leaving and how these motivations impact their lives and emotional well-being.

Fear of the Unknown

One of the strongest reasons people stay in relationships despite unhappiness is the fear of the unknown. Stepping into a life without a partner can feel like venturing into uncharted territory, especially if the relationship has been a long one.

This fear often stems from the security that comes with routine, even if that routine isn't fulfilling.

For many, the thought of starting over, potentially facing loneliness, judgment, or uncertainty, can seem scarier than staying in a relationship that's familiar but unloving.

The unknown can include worries about how life might change socially, financially, or emotionally.

Many people ask themselves:

Will I be able to manage on my own?

Will I find someone else?

Will I regret leaving?

These questions can cloud judgment, causing a person to settle for a situation that, while not ideal, feels safer than risking the potential discomforts of independence. This type of fear often becomes a paralyzing force, making the familiar feel like the only viable option.

Financial Security and Practical Concerns

Leaving a relationship isn't just emotionally challenging; it also brings practical considerations, particularly around financial security.

Financial dependency is a common reason people stay, especially in relationships where one partner may have relied on the other for financial support.

When a person has shared expenses, joint assets, or is dependent on a partner's income, the prospect of leaving can bring fears of economic hardship or loss of lifestyle.

These practical concerns are especially true for individuals who may have put their careers on hold for family or focused their energy on shared goals within the relationship.

In situations where one partner has assumed a more traditional homemaking role or sacrificed career growth, the loss of that shared financial base can feel insurmountable.

Questions about living arrangements, division of assets, or the ability to meet daily expenses can overshadow the need for emotional well-being.

Moreover, the cost of separation itself, moving expenses, legal fees, or financial settlements, can be overwhelming. It's no surprise that many people stay because the idea of financial instability looms too large, and the realities of navigating these logistics are too daunting.

In these cases, the decision to stay is often viewed as a matter of survival, outweighing the emotional costs of remaining.

Comfort in Familiarity: The Trap of Routine

Comfort, often mistaken for contentment, can be one of the trickiest reasons for staying in a loveless relationship. After years or even decades together, many couples fall into routines that provide a sense of predictability and stability, even if they lack intimacy or passion.

This comfort, while surface-level, can make leaving feel unnecessary or like too much effort. The familiarity of routines, traditions, and shared history can create a powerful bond, even if that bond is built more on habit than on love.

Leaving would mean breaking away from a life that's been built together, with memories and shared experiences that feel like they define both partners. There's a comfort in waking up and knowing what to expect each day, in knowing someone's habits, or even in the rituals of shared meals or small daily routines.

Disrupting these patterns can feel not only like a loss of a relationship but a loss of a whole way of life. This attachment to the comfort of the known often leads people to justify staying, choosing stability over emotional fulfillment.

For many, the idea of re-establishing a new life without these routines is too intimidating.

The thought of having to start over, form new habits, and perhaps even face judgment from others can make staying in the relationship feel like the path of least resistance.

Social Pressures and Fear of Judgment

Social expectations and the fear of judgment play a huge role in why many people stay in relationships that no longer bring them happiness.

Society often upholds ideals of long-term commitment, portraying enduring relationships as symbols of strength, resilience, and even moral character. People may fear that leaving will be seen as a failure or as giving up, which can feel like a personal defeat in the eyes of others.

Family and friends may also add to this pressure, offering unsolicited opinions or even condemning the idea of separation. For individuals with children, the concern about how others might view them as parents, or fears of impacting their children's lives can be overwhelming.

In these cases, a person might feel that the judgment and shame associated with leaving are too much to bear, even if they're suffering within the relationship. They may stay to avoid uncomfortable questions or perceived disappointment from those around them, prioritizing social acceptance over their own happiness.

Guilt and Responsibility

The sense of responsibility toward a partner is often a powerful reason people don't leave. In relationships, especially those with a long history, there's often a feeling of duty or guilt tied to leaving a partner, particularly if that partner is emotionally or financially dependent.

People may feel a strong responsibility to stay, worrying that leaving would leave their partner in a vulnerable position.

This sense of duty can be magnified if one partner is dealing with personal challenges like mental health struggles, financial hardships, or even physical health issues.

Individuals may stay out of compassion, believing that their leaving would be selfish or cause additional harm. They may feel morally or ethically obligated to stay, even if it means sacrificing their own well-being.

The weight of responsibility can make it difficult to separate self-care from perceived selfishness. People in this position often question whether their own happiness justifies the impact that leaving would have on their partner. This guilt can become a significant emotional anchor, keeping them tied to a relationship that has long ceased to be fulfilling.

Hope for Change and Fear of Regret

Many people stay in relationships because they hold on to the hope that things might improve. This hope may be fueled by memories of happier times, promises of change, or small gestures that hint at a possible shift in the relationship dynamic.

The belief that "things might get better" can be enough to justify staying, even if evidence suggests otherwise. Individuals may tell themselves that with enough time, effort, or patience, the relationship could return to what it once was.

Alongside hope, there is also the fear of regret. Leaving is a monumental decision, and the fear of looking back with regret can make staying feel like the safer choice. People might worry that they'll miss the security or companionship of their partner or that they'll look back and question if leaving was the right move. This fear of regret keeps them in a place of inaction, afraid that they may lose something valuable that they can't yet see.

The Psychological Comfort of Avoiding Change

Finally, the psychological comfort of avoiding change is one of the most common reasons people remain in unsatisfying relationships. Change, by nature, brings a level of discomfort and uncertainty, and humans are wired to resist it.

People often choose the path of least resistance to avoid the stress and potential upheaval that change entails. This aversion to change can override the desire for happiness or self-fulfillment, keeping them in a situation that feels "good enough" or "not that bad."

The psychological safety of staying, even if unfulfilling, is often preferred over the anxiety of navigating a new chapter alone. This choice reflects the mental process of self-preservation, where the fear of confronting new challenges outweighs the discomfort of the current situation.

In this chapter, we've explored the complex factors that keep people in relationships that no longer bring fulfillment. The fear of the unknown, financial dependence, comfort in routine, social pressures, guilt, hope for change, and the desire to avoid change are all powerful forces that shape this choice.

By examining these motivations, individuals can better understand the deep-seated reasons that make leaving feel difficult, allowing them to make informed decisions about whether to stay or seek a new path forward. Recognizing these patterns is the first step toward reclaiming self-agency and building the courage to make choices that align with one's well-being.

"Nowhere Else to Go" – Lisa, Age 61

When Lisa's last child moved out, she felt the silence like a slap. Her marriage to Paul had always been distant, but with no kids to fill the gaps, the emptiness became unbearable. Still, she stayed.

Why?

"Because I didn't know what else to do," she confessed. "I hadn't worked in years. My name wasn't on the house. Where would I go?

Who would I be?" Fear of starting over kept her frozen in a life that no longer fit. But the familiarity, even if loveless, felt safer than the unknown.

Can you relate to any part of this story?

What would reclaiming your voice look like today, even in a small way?

"Love's Gone—Now What's Left of You?"

Chapter 5: Realizing It's Too Late: When the Window to Leave Closes

In every relationship, there's a delicate tipping point where the choice to leave, once fully open, slowly closes.

This chapter delves into the painful realization that, for some, the window of opportunity to leave has faded, either because circumstances have changed, life responsibilities have grown heavier, or the sense of self-worth and confidence has diminished over time.

This sense of "too late" doesn't always mean it's impossible to leave, but it often feels that way, creating emotional and mental barriers that make separation seem insurmountable.

Whether it's the weight of age, the deep-seated patterns that have formed over the years, or the fear that leaving now would carry too high a price, this chapter examines how people come to realize they may have stayed too long and what it means to confront that reality.

How Time Changes Us: From Passionate Love to Resigned Coexistence

Relationships go through natural cycles. Most people start with a phase of intense connection, where dreams are shared, passions are high, and a future together feels assured. Over time, as people grow, adapt, or face life's challenges, the relationship often shifts as well.

If the relationship begins to stagnate, it's easy to tell oneself that it's just a phase, believing the intensity will return eventually. But sometimes, instead of circling back to happiness, people find themselves growing increasingly apart, moving from passionate love to a resigned coexistence.

As years pass, we also find that the expectations we had when we were younger may not align with where we are now. In some relationships, this disparity becomes glaring, yet the thought of change seems far too overwhelming.

The idea of leaving shifts from a real possibility to a hypothetical one, a dream deferred. Realizing that time has altered not just the relationship but the people in it can lead to the painful understanding that life is not what it once was and that the time to leave may have quietly slipped away.

A Loss of Independence and Self-Identity

One of the most challenging aspects of staying in a relationship too long is the gradual erosion of independence and self-identity. In many cases, people in long-term, unhappy relationships adapt to fit their partner's world, compromising so often that they no longer recognize who they are apart from the relationship.

This loss of individuality can make leaving feel impossible because they're unsure who they would even be without the other person.

As time passes, a sense of self-worth often diminishes, replaced by self-doubt and a fear of inadequacy. The idea of being alone can feel not only daunting but almost unnatural, as though they're leaving part of themselves behind.

By the time they realize it, years of conforming to the needs and desires of the relationship have taken their toll, making them feel that their identity is so intertwined with their partner's that breaking away would leave them hollow or adrift.

This fear of losing oneself entirely can keep people rooted in relationships, even when they know deep down that they're no longer happy.

Increased Dependence on Shared Resources and Routines

As relationships grow in length, so do the shared responsibilities and resources. Years of financial, emotional, and logistical integration create a sense of dependence that can feel nearly impossible to unravel.

Financial commitments such as joint property, shared bank accounts, or mutual debts add complexity to the decision to separate.

The more intertwined lives become, the harder it is to imagine dividing them without losing stability, security, or comfort.

This increased dependence isn't just financial; it's practical. There's a comfort in the routines, daily rituals, and responsibilities shared between partners, even if those routines are no longer fulfilling.

By the time someone realizes they want to leave, the amount of shared commitments, like children, family obligations, or social connections, may feel like insurmountable obstacles, making departure seem impractical and even reckless.

Over time, these responsibilities become like anchors, holding people back from making a choice they might have once believed possible.

Health and Age: The Impact of Physical and Emotional Wear

For many, age plays a significant role in the feeling that the window to leave has closed. As people grow older, health issues may arise, or energy and resilience may dwindle.

Physical limitations or the natural aging process can make the prospect of starting over seem not only daunting but possibly unfeasible. The perception that they are "too old" to begin anew can weigh heavily, reinforcing the belief that they missed the opportunity for change and that leaving now might be impractical or unwise.

Emotionally, the strain of a long, unfulfilling relationship also takes a toll, wearing down a person's resilience and confidence.

By the time they consider leaving, their ability to imagine a different life may feel diminished, replaced by the fear that they no longer have the strength to go through the process of separation.

This perception is compounded by societal narratives about "aging gracefully" or "growing old together," which can make the decision to leave feel counter to the expected life path.

The emotional and physical toll of age can transform the concept of leaving from a choice into a distant, unrealistic dream.

The Impact of Children and Family Ties

The presence of children is often a powerful factor that keeps people in relationships they otherwise might leave. Children bring a sense of responsibility that can create a profound commitment to staying, even in an unloving relationship.

Many people stay for the sake of their children's stability or to avoid disrupting family life, reasoning that it's better for the children if both parents remain together, regardless of their own happiness.

As children grow, however, new complications arise. Parents may feel that the years invested "for the children's sake" are now impossible to recover, creating a sense of having sacrificed too much to leave.

In addition, when children grow up and leave home, some partners may feel a renewed sense of emptiness, questioning whether the relationship ever had a foundation beyond parenting.

But by then, they may feel that too much time has passed to make a different choice, resigned to a life where the opportunity to leave has closed, and they must now make the best of the situation.

Emotional Attachment to the Past: Living on Memories

Another reason the window to leave can feel closed is the emotional attachment to memories and shared experiences. Even in a relationship where love has faded, the past remains: memories of better times, shared milestones, and a history that defines both partners. For many, this attachment to the past can create a powerful emotional barrier, making it difficult to let go, even when the present offers little fulfillment.

There's a reluctance to "abandon" the life they've built, as it represents not just years, but an identity forged through shared experiences.

Letting go can feel like erasing the value of all those years, causing a deep sense of loss and fear that life might feel empty or devoid of meaning without those memories.

This nostalgia, though it may be tied to a faded love, keeps people emotionally anchored to a relationship that they otherwise know isn't healthy.

Accepting "Good Enough" as the New Normal

Perhaps one of the most common realizations is the acceptance of "good enough" as the new normal.

After years of unmet needs and unrealized dreams within a relationship, many come to a point where they adjust their expectations.

They tell themselves that this is what life is: less about fulfillment and more about getting by. They rationalize the situation by convincing themselves that no relationship is perfect, and that "good enough" is all they need to be content.

In this state, the idea of leaving becomes less about seeking happiness and more about simply avoiding disruption. They've come to terms with the compromises, choosing stability over the pursuit of joy.

 In a way, they've redefined what they need to survive, even if it falls short of what they once desired. Over time, "good enough" becomes the mantra, a way to shield themselves from the pain of realizing that the opportunity for happiness, which might have existed in the past, has now faded.

In this chapter, we explored the various reasons people come to believe the window for leaving has closed, from health concerns and financial dependence to emotional attachment and the impact of age.

While the realization that it's "too late" is deeply personal, the factors behind it are often universal.

By understanding these influences, individuals may come to see their situation more clearly, identifying the barriers that hold them in place and determining if, indeed, the door has fully closed or if there remains a way to move forward.

This chapter serves as a sobering reminder of how time, choices, and unspoken fears shape the lives we ultimately choose to live.

"The Clock Ran Out" – Thomas, Age 70

Thomas thought he'd leave after retirement.

He even had a secret savings account. But then his wife got sick.

Then his knees started acting up. Then the pandemic hit. Suddenly, the years were gone.

Now in his seventies, Thomas quietly regrets staying in a marriage that lost its joy decades ago. "I always thought there'd be time," he said, "but now I'm too tired. Too set in the routine. I stayed for the comfort, but lost my chance at freedom."

Can you relate to any part of this story?

What would reclaiming your voice look like today, even in a small way?

"Rediscovering yourself when the relationship is empty."

Chapter 6: Finding Strength in Resilience: Making the Best of What's Left

In relationships where love has faded and leaving feels impossible or unrealistic, finding a path forward requires a new kind of strength. In these situations, resilience becomes a lifeline, offering a way to endure and, ultimately, rediscover purpose and self-worth, even within an unfulfilling relationship.

This chapter explores how individuals find inner strength by focusing on self-care, re-evaluating their values, and seeking small sources of personal joy and fulfillment. It is about learning to thrive despite circumstances and transforming the space once reserved for romantic love into something that sustains and uplifts.

Embracing Acceptance: Releasing the Ideal and Embracing Reality

One of the first steps toward resilience is coming to terms with the reality of the situation. Often, people remain in a relationship expecting that it will somehow return to what it once was.

However, clinging to that ideal only creates disappointment, stress, and an endless cycle of unmet expectations.

Finding resilience requires releasing the notion of what the relationship "should" be and accepting it as it is.

Acceptance does not mean giving up on happiness or settling for a life of dissatisfaction. Instead, it's about releasing the need for external validation from the relationship and finding peace in the present.

Many find that embracing reality offers an unexpected sense of relief, freeing them from the emotional turmoil of hoping for change. By focusing on what they can control, their thoughts, feelings, and actions, they create a foundation for inner peace that no longer relies on their partner.

This mindset shift enables them to approach their life with a clearer sense of what they can achieve independently of the relationship.

Cultivating Self-Care and Rediscovering Personal Joy

When love fades in a relationship, individuals often lose sight of their own needs, sacrificing self-care in favor of their partner's expectations or relationship routines.

Reclaiming strength involves making self-care a priority and rediscovering joy outside of the partnership. This can mean dedicating time to hobbies, exploring creative outlets, or pursuing interests that may have been put aside.

Self-care extends beyond physical well-being to include mental and emotional health as well. Activities like journaling, meditation, and regular exercise become crucial tools for maintaining balance.

Many find that reintroducing self-care routines, no matter how small, becomes an anchor; a way to stay centered and grounded amidst the challenges of an unsatisfying relationship.

Over time, these routines foster a renewed sense of self, helping individuals tap into their inherent strength and reminding them that they are more than their relationship.

Finding small personal joys is equally important. It might be a walk in the park, a day spent reading, or moments of solitude in a quiet space.

These instances of happiness don't require approval or recognition from their partner; they are purely for themselves. This shift from relying on the relationship for happiness to creating personal fulfillment is a powerful act of resilience.

It is a declaration that their well-being and happiness remain priorities, despite the limitations of their relationship.

Setting Boundaries and Reclaiming Personal Space

For many people in strained relationships, boundaries have become blurred over the years, contributing to feelings of resentment, frustration, and even loss of self.

Setting boundaries can be an essential act of self-preservation, even within the context of a loveless relationship. Boundaries serve as a form of self-respect, defining what they will and won't accept, allowing them to protect their emotional and mental space.

Re-establishing boundaries could involve carving out dedicated time for themselves, asking for respect regarding personal choices, or simply ensuring that their needs are recognized.

Although boundaries might initially be met with resistance, they serve as a reminder of personal autonomy and agency. By reclaiming personal space within the relationship, they begin to reassert their identity. This process allows them to feel more empowered and resilient, knowing that they have established limits that honor their self-worth, regardless of the nature of their partnership.

For those who may struggle with asserting boundaries, small steps can lead to significant change. This might mean creating a personal schedule or setting aside time where they engage in activities independently.

Even though the changes might feel subtle, these boundaries foster a sense of independence, which strengthens the resilience needed to thrive in an unfulfilling relationship.

Building a Support System Outside the Relationship

Resilience is often strengthened by the people around us, and a key aspect of finding strength in a loveless relationship is cultivating a support system beyond the partnership.

This network could include friends, family members, or even support groups where they can share experiences and gain insights without fear of judgment.

Building a support system doesn't necessarily mean seeking advice about leaving or changing the relationship; it's about having people who can offer encouragement and empathy.

A trusted friend, family member, or counselor can provide perspective and remind them of their worth, helping them navigate the complex emotions of staying. By having this outlet, they feel less isolated and more equipped to face the challenges that arise within the relationship.

Engaging in community or volunteering activities can also offer a sense of purpose and belonging.

Helping others can be a powerful way to reframe their own experiences and recognize the value they bring to the world. As they establish connections outside the relationship, they create emotional and social buffers that offer comfort and stability.

Finding Purpose and Meaning Beyond the Relationship

A significant aspect of resilience is finding purpose beyond the confines of the relationship. For many, a loveless partnership becomes bearable when they focus on meaningful goals that inspire them.

This can involve professional growth, personal development, or pursuing a passion project that has long been set aside.

Discovering purpose beyond the relationship is both liberating and grounding. It allows them to invest in their future independently of the relationship, giving them a reason to look forward to each day with renewed optimism.

They might consider learning a new skill, furthering their education, or dedicating themselves to a cause they believe in. By building a life rich with meaning, they develop resilience as well as a sense of accomplishment and pride that remains theirs, independent of their partner's recognition or approval.

Finding purpose also nurtures a sense of identity, affirming that they are not defined solely by their relationship status but by their talents, values, and contributions. In doing so, they create a legacy of resilience and fulfillment that can offer comfort, even within challenging circumstances.

Practicing Gratitude and Focusing on the Positives

In challenging relationships, it's easy to focus on what's lacking, which can amplify feelings of frustration and resentment. However, practicing gratitude has been shown to enhance resilience by fostering a more balanced outlook.

While it may feel difficult to appreciate aspects of a relationship that's no longer fulfilling, gratitude isn't about ignoring challenges but rather recognizing the good that still exists.

This gratitude practice might include small acts of kindness their partner still shows, qualities they respect in their partner, or shared life experiences that have added richness to their lives.

In addition, focusing on aspects of their own life that bring them joy, fulfillment, or comfort fosters a more positive mindset. By shifting focus toward gratitude, they build emotional resilience, allowing them to better manage the less satisfying parts of their relationship.

Gratitude also opens the door to self-compassion. By acknowledging the challenges they face without judgment, they can find peace in their resilience and perseverance.

This practice encourages them to celebrate their ability to endure, adapt, and grow, honoring the strength it takes to make the best of what's left.

Developing a Resilience-Based Mindset: Embracing Growth Through Challenges

Ultimately, resilience involves viewing challenges as opportunities for growth. Within the context of a loveless relationship, this means shifting from a mindset of endurance to one of personal development.

By redefining their experience as one of strength rather than limitation, they can foster a deeper appreciation for their capacity to adapt and thrive.

A resilience-based mindset also acknowledges the learning gained through difficulty. It's not about denying the hardship but recognizing the lessons about patience, self-worth, and inner strength that have emerged over time.

This growth-oriented perspective can foster a sense of fulfillment even within a stagnant relationship, affirming that they are more than their circumstances.

Developing resilience doesn't happen overnight, but with each step, whether it's establishing boundaries, cultivating joy, or building support, they move closer to creating a life filled with purpose and contentment.

This shift empowers them to redefine what fulfillment means on their terms, embracing their ability to find strength, meaning, and even hope in what's left.

In this Chapter, we explored how resilience serves as a foundation for finding peace and purpose within a loveless relationship. From setting boundaries and nurturing self-care to cultivating gratitude and purpose outside the relationship, these strategies empower individuals to find strength within themselves.

This chapter underscores that resilience isn't merely about enduring hardship but transforming it into a life enriched by self-respect, joy, and meaning. Through resilience, they learn to embrace their journey with acceptance and courage, finding contentment even amidst challenging circumstances.

"Room of Her Own" – Evelyn, Age 68

Evelyn didn't leave her husband, but she stopped living for him.

After 40 years together, many of them cold, she finally claimed the guest room as her own space.

She redecorated it with lavender curtains, soft lights, books, and music. It became her sanctuary. "He still watches TV alone," she said, "but now I write. I read. I light candles. I don't wait for him to see me anymore.

I see myself." Evelyn redefined what it meant to survive—on her terms.

Can you relate to any part of this story?

What would reclaiming your voice look like today, even in a small way?

Chapter 7: A New Kind of Freedom: Reclaiming Self-Worth and Inner Peace

In the final chapter, we explore the concept of freedom that goes beyond leaving or staying in a relationship. This freedom involves reclaiming self-worth, cultivating inner peace, and redefining happiness on one's terms.

In a loveless relationship, true freedom comes from finding peace and value within oneself, irrespective of the limitations posed by the relationship. By rediscovering personal worth and achieving inner balance, individuals learn to live with a renewed sense of self.

This freedom offers a profound form of strength and independence, even when the external circumstances remain the same.

Rediscovering Self-Worth: Realizing You Are More Than Your Relationship

One of the greatest challenges in a stagnant relationship is the gradual erosion of self-worth. Many people internalize the lack of love or respect from their partner, leading them to question their value.

Rediscovering self-worth is essential to reclaiming freedom, as it empowers individuals to recognize that they are worthy of love, respect, and happiness, regardless of how their partner views or treats them.

Rediscovering self-worth involves a journey inward, asking, "Who am I apart from this relationship?" and "What do I deserve?"

It may be helpful to reflect on past accomplishments, personal strengths, or times they overcame adversity. This helps remind them of their resilience and worthiness, independent of the relationship.

This process can also include affirmations, journaling, or consulting with trusted friends who can provide an honest and loving perspective.

Over time, the realization that self-worth doesn't rely on external validation, especially from a partner, helps individuals feel liberated from needing approval or validation. This reclaims a sense of dignity and pride that re-establishes one's identity outside of the relationship.

Focusing on Inner Peace: Creating a Calm Sanctuary Within

Inner peace is not dependent on external conditions; it is something cultivated from within. For many people in unsatisfying relationships, a lack of inner peace can manifest as chronic stress, anxiety, or feelings of hopelessness.

However, finding peace within allows individuals to anchor themselves, regardless of the circumstances.

Developing inner peace can start with mindfulness practices, such as meditation, breathing exercises, or simply taking time each day to be still.

These practices help create mental and emotional space, allowing them to detach from the negativity that may surround them and refocus on what truly matters.

Inner peace doesn't necessarily mean feeling happy all the time; it's about finding a state of calm and acceptance that allows one to remain centered even when challenges arise.

Creating a personal sanctuary, either mentally or physically, can also foster inner peace. This could be a physical space where they can unwind, such as a favorite chair or room in the house, or a mental refuge they create through visualization.

Taking time each day to connect with this "safe place" encourages feelings of tranquility and reminds them that peace is always accessible.

With inner peace comes the strength to face each day with calmness and clarity, free from the emotional turmoil that often accompanies strained relationships.

Finding New Purpose and Personal Goals

A significant aspect of reclaiming self-worth is finding purpose and setting personal goals that reignite passion and joy. Many people in long-term, loveless relationships often let go of their ambitions, feeling that their dreams are either irrelevant or unattainable.

However, reclaiming a sense of purpose reminds individuals that they are capable of growth and fulfillment, regardless of their relationship status.

To begin, they might reflect on interests or dreams that were once meaningful. This might be a hobby, a professional pursuit, or a community project that has long been set aside.

By gradually re-engaging with these passions, they create a sense of personal satisfaction and purpose. Setting goals, however small, gives life a new direction, reminding them that their story continues, with or without a fulfilling romantic relationship.

As they pursue these goals, they develop a renewed sense of identity based on their talents, values, and contributions. This feeling of purpose serves as a stabilizing force, reaffirming that they have something valuable to offer the world.

 They may even discover new passions or talents, uncovering parts of themselves that had been dormant. This reawakening offers a new kind of freedom—the freedom to define who they are and what they want out of life.

Building Independence: Financial, Emotional, and Social Autonomy

Freedom often goes hand-in-hand with independence, and one of the most empowering steps in reclaiming self-worth and inner peace is building a foundation of autonomy.

Independence can take many forms, but financial, emotional, and social independence are particularly powerful.

Financial independence may be challenging in certain relationships, especially when resources are shared. However, taking steps toward financial autonomy, even small ones, fosters a sense of security and control.

Whether it's budgeting, saving, or finding ways to generate additional income, financial independence allows individuals to feel more empowered, capable of supporting themselves without relying on their partner.

This shift in power dynamics fosters greater self-worth, as they realize that they are capable of standing on their own.

Emotional independence involves reducing reliance on a partner for validation, comfort, or happiness. While relationships often foster emotional interdependence, loveless relationships can drain emotional reserves without offering support in return.

By practicing self-compassion, managing their emotions, and finding support outside the relationship, individuals begin to build emotional resilience. This independence encourages them to rely on themselves for validation, giving them the strength to remain balanced regardless of their partner's actions.

Social independence is equally valuable. Developing friendships, joining groups, or participating in community events fosters a strong support network outside the relationship. This creates a sense of connection and belonging, providing emotional nourishment that the relationship may no longer offer.

These friendships can offer inspiration, encouragement, and a sense of unity that supports their journey toward self-worth and inner peace.

Letting Go of Resentment and Embracing Forgiveness

In loveless relationships, feelings of resentment can build over time, creating emotional barriers that inhibit peace. Reclaiming inner freedom means finding a way to release these negative emotions, as holding onto resentment often hurts the person more than anyone else. Forgiveness becomes an act of self-liberation, allowing individuals to move forward without carrying the weight of past grievances.

Forgiveness doesn't mean condoning hurtful behavior or forgetting past wrongs; rather, it involves letting go of the desire to dwell on these events. It is an internal process, freeing them from the emotional burden that resentment brings.

This can take time, and it may involve forgiveness not only of the partner but of oneself for any perceived mistakes or missed opportunities.

Through forgiveness, they find the emotional space to focus on growth rather than lingering pain.

It becomes a way to reclaim power, as they are no longer controlled by past hurts. By letting go of resentment, they embrace a sense of lightness and peace that restores their inner freedom and allows them to approach life with a renewed sense of optimism.

Celebrating Personal Growth and Small Wins

An essential aspect of reclaiming self-worth and inner peace is recognizing progress and celebrating small victories. As individuals navigate the journey toward freedom within a loveless relationship, they are bound to face challenges.

By acknowledging each small step, whether it's setting a boundary, practicing self-care, or making time for a hobby, they validate their efforts and reinforce their sense of worth.

Celebrating growth, no matter how small, helps them maintain momentum and prevents them from feeling stagnant. These "small wins" serve as a reminder of their resilience and perseverance, showing that they are capable of making positive changes despite their circumstances.

Over time, these victories add up, creating a cumulative sense of achievement that enhances self-worth and builds a foundation of inner peace.

This practice of recognizing progress fosters a growth mindset, encouraging them to view their journey as a continuous process of self-discovery and improvement.

Each step forward becomes a testament to their strength, reminding them that freedom and fulfillment come from within.

This final chapter explores the journey to a new kind of freedom; one found in reclaiming self-worth and cultivating inner peace within a loveless relationship. Through accepting reality, nurturing inner peace, building independence, and releasing resentment, individuals learn to thrive despite challenging circumstances.

This chapter highlights the transformative power of self-compassion, resilience, and personal growth, demonstrating that true freedom comes from within.

By embracing this new sense of autonomy and self-respect, they find strength, purpose, and peace, creating a life that reflects their inherent worth and resilience.

"Choosing Herself Again" – Monique, Age 45

Monique didn't leave physically, yet. But emotionally, she's building a life beyond the marriage.

She's going back to school, she started a blog, and she meets with friends twice a month for brunch and laughs. "I realized that staying doesn't have to mean staying stuck," she shared.

"I'm finally choosing me. Maybe I'll leave one day. Maybe I won't. But either way, I've already started living again."

Can you relate to any part of this story?

What would reclaiming your voice look like today, even in a small way?

"Freedom Isn't Always Leaving—Sometimes It's Staying Unbroken"

Reflection Page

A Quiet Moment with Yourself

As you close these pages, take a moment to check in, not with the relationship, but with you.

What did you learn about yourself as you read this book?

What emotions came up that you've long buried or avoided?

What would reclaiming your peace look like in your current life?

You may not have all the answers right now, and that's okay. But what you do have is awareness. And from awareness, change is always possible. Whether you choose to stay, go, or simply breathe differently, let it be from a place of worthiness, not shame or guilt.

This is not the end of your story. It's the beginning of the part where you start choosing yourself again.

Write one promise to yourself here:

Research and Sources

In crafting After the Love is Gone, I have drawn on a blend of research, expert insights, and real-life stories to provide a comprehensive understanding of the complexities and resilience involved in navigating loveless relationships. This book is grounded in evidence-based information from relationship psychology, personal development, and mental health studies. Below, I've listed some of the primary fields, sources, and research that informed the ideas and guidance in this book.

Relationship and Attachment Theory

Several concepts discussed here are informed by attachment theory and relationship psychology, which explore how individuals form, maintain, and end relationships. Researchers like Dr. John Bowlby and Dr. Mary Ainsworth have extensively studied attachment, while Dr. John Gottman's work provides insights into marital stability and the dynamics of long-term relationships.

Mental Health and Emotional Resilience

Understanding the mental and emotional toll of remaining in challenging relationships is essential to this topic. Research by psychologists such as Dr. Brené Brown on vulnerability and resilience, as well as studies on emotional regulation and mindfulness from authors like Dr. Kristin Neff, has greatly informed the book's approach to coping with adverse relational dynamics.

Self-Worth and Personal Empowerment

Themes around self-worth and reclaiming identity are informed by self-compassion research and personal empowerment studies. Dr. Nathaniel Branden's work on self-esteem, combined with insights from cognitive-behavioral therapy (CBT) practices, sheds light on the importance of nurturing self-compassion and personal empowerment, even in unsupportive environments.

Mindfulness and Inner Peace

Achieving inner peace while remaining in a difficult relationship is rooted in mindfulness practices. Techniques and ideas from the work of Dr. Jon Kabat-Zinn, founder of Mindfulness-Based Stress Reduction (MBSR), provide a foundation for finding calm and resilience. Additionally, books on mindfulness and mental clarity by Thich Nhat Hanh influenced the approaches shared in the book.

Personal Stories and Case Studies

The experiences and challenges of individuals navigating loveless relationships are referenced throughout the book, reflecting common struggles and triumphs. These stories are adapted for privacy but draw from real-life scenarios shared through interviews, social research, and counseling anecdotes to provide a genuine, relatable context.

Helpful Resources

If you're ready to dive deeper into your healing journey, here are books, websites, and support tools that can help you process, grow, and rebuild:

Books

The Dance of Intimacy by Dr. Harriet Lerner

Too Good to Leave, Too Bad to Stay by Mira Kirshenbaum

Set Boundaries, Find Peace by Nedra Glover Tawwab

Radical Acceptance by Tara Brach

The Gifts of Imperfection by Brené Brown

Podcasts & Online Support

Therapy Chat with Laura Reagan

Where Should We Begin? with Esther Perel

The Love, Happiness, and Success Podcast

www.psychologytoday.com — Find a therapist by location

www.talkspace.com — Online therapy access

Self-Care & Empowerment Tools

Journaling apps: Day One, Journey, Reflectly

Meditation apps: Calm, Headspace, Insight Timer

Local or virtual support groups for women, partners, or those in long-term caregiving relationships (check Meetup, Facebook Groups, or local community centers)

Why I Wrote This Book

The journey of love isn't always straightforward, nor is it always fulfilling. This book was born from a place of empathy and understanding, having seen so many around me, and perhaps at times even myself, struggle in relationships that had lost their spark, yet remained out of practicality, fear, or uncertainty.

After the Love is Gone is for anyone who has ever questioned their own strength, for those who felt trapped by love's absence and burdened by the decisions that followed.

I wrote this book to provide a guide, a gentle companion, and perhaps a bit of solace for those seeking a way to navigate the quiet complexities of a loveless relationship. May it serve as a reminder that your worth is not defined by the state of your relationship, and that inner peace is possible, even within difficult circumstances.

Stay Connected with Me

This isn't goodbye. This is just the beginning.

If this book spoke to your soul, I invite you to join my inner circle, a place for women (and men) who are ready to grow, heal, and walk in truth together.

✉ Subscribe to the "Letters from vgdawson" Newsletter

Get exclusive reflections, behind-the-scenes writing updates, journal prompts, book releases, and self-care tools delivered straight to your inbox.

📫 Sign up at: www.what2buynext.com/newsletter

📱 Follow on Social Media:

Instagram | YouTube | TikTok: @what2buynext

Website: www.what2buynext.com

Together, let's keep writing new chapters.

Chapters of peace, purpose, and power.

You deserve every bit of it.

Warmly, *Vgdawson*

Thank You

To everyone who takes the time to read these pages, thank you.

Writing this book has been a journey of reflection, and I am honored to have the opportunity to share it with you.

If you find strength, understanding, or even a little bit of hope here, then this book has achieved its purpose.

Thank you for joining me on this journey, for allowing me to be part of yours, and for trusting in the process of finding strength where it may seem hidden.

My wish is that this book or eBook serves as a beacon of resilience, offering you comfort and courage as you navigate your own path.

Inspired by Vgdawson

WHAT2BUYNEXT BOOKSHELF
&
LIFE CHOICES CANDLE COMPANY

Every story I write — and every candle I create — comes from one simple truth: we all need reminders of our strength, our worth, and our ability to begin again.
Read with purpose. Reflect with peace. Live with intention.

Then, set the mood for your reading journey with my Essence Candle Collection — each scent inspired by a book, each flame a symbol of healing and hope.

Find everything at www.what2buynext.com

The Essence Collection by vgdawson
Light a candle. Open a book.
Begin again.

Living on Purpose

Mood: Energizing • Balanced • Confident

An uplifting citrus scent to inspire motivation and creativity. The perfect companion while journaling or reading something that challenges you to grow.

"I am evolving into the best version of me."

Hand-poured in the USA • Natural Soy Wax

Find everything at www.what2buynext.com

www.ingramcontent.com/pod-product-compliance
Lightning Source LLC
Chambersburg PA
CBHW050036040726
47599CB00015B/1703